D1208032

EX LIBRIS
R.C. ELLIS
SOUTH ORANGE
PUBLIC LIBRARY

The Unicorns

BY HELGA SANDBURG

The Wheel of Earth
Measure My Love
The Owl's Roost
Sweet Music
The Unicorns

CHILDREN'S BOOKS

Blueberry
Joel and the Wild Goose
Gingerbread
Bo and the Old Donkey

THE UNICORNS

by

Helga Sandburg

THE DIAL PRESS • 1965 • NEW YORK

Library of Congress Catalog Card Number: 65-15328
MANUFACTURED IN THE UNITED STATES OF AMERICA

FOR MY HUSBAND,

Barney Crile

Contents

Foreword

The poet is always bursting with news—good, bad, seldom indifferent. All his work is autobiographical. To him everything under the sun is new. The poet is in love with words, engrossed in a lifelong affair with his language. He is bent upon perfection of expression, remembering Corinthians I, 14th Chapter, 9th Verse: "So likewise ye, except ye utter by the tongue words easy to be understood, how shall it be known what is spoken? for ye shall speak into the air."

The poet, in order to be fertile, is busy looking over forbears, one, Mr. Whitman instructing:

> This is what you shall do: love the earth and sun and animals, despise riches, give alms to everyone that asks, stand up for the stupid and crazy, devote your income and labor to others, hate tyrants, argue not concerning God, have patience and indulgence toward the people, take off your hat to nothing known or unknown or to any man or number of men, go freely with powerful uneducated persons and with the young and with the mothers of families, read in the open air, re-examine all you have been told at school or church or in any book, dismiss whatever insults your soul.

The poet is off in his corner now. He gazes out of the window, not hearing the traffic below or the whistle of the bird. The curtains stir and he doesn't feel the wind at all. He doesn't hear his name being called. When his spouse or child or mother appears in the doorway, it seems as if he is daydreaming, idle. But his mind is stirring in an inexorable pattern. In a while he will turn concentrated to his pencil and paper.

The poet Mr. Sandburg, back nearly fifty years, when reviewing his contemporary, Mr. Pound, said, "People write poetry because they want to . . . it is the dark stuff of life that comes and goes." And it is true.

HELGA SANDBURG
June 1964
Cleveland, Ohio

The Unicorns

(For B.C.)

Why, my dear, almost at dawn now, when the light
Is a little like twilight, does a mourning dove
Mourn through the stone branches of the buildings
Of this town? Why, in the streets below, do the hooves
        sound
Of a snow-white unicorn stepping by, he who is
Love And Disaster, hoping to be seen and known?
Why, my darling, is this the hour of births of children
And goings of lovers and prayers of disciples?
Why, in the countryside now does there ring a noise
Like bells tolled from farm to farm, as the roosters,
The red-capped dawn boys, stand strained
On scalèd legs, and in strange unholy voices proclaim
All the unicorns walking in the lanes and ways?
Why, when I run from you, my dear, and down the stair
And follow him to announce that I see and recognize,
Does he turn his pale blue eyes on me and frown
And leap and clatter away as the dove's cry mourns
And dawn breaks red over the old buildings of the street?

Sin

Nevertheless I killed them one and one.
It's no excuse that I was somewhat young
Or that they stole the grain in my father's barn.
As each reared its head I shot it down.
Some of them must have had nests somewhere,
And some of them must have been starting to pair;
Certainly there was grain enough to share!

Their eyes were jewels, hot and black.
I looked, and innocent they looked back.
Each crossed its hands at its furry breast
And with father's rifle I did the rest.
From those days to these are long years between.
I had disremembered, but now begin to dream,
Repenting my deeds at age thirteen.

Éloge to My Mother

This small-boned powerful life-loving woman
Views the world and us her children introspectively.
With disheveled chatter and disposition even
To us she is certain sanctuary.

And when she goes with odorous straw to make
A bed for those small goats she loves,
They fall kneeling among her beautiful hands that take
Strongly apart the oat bales interwove.

They adore her! And when they set about
To drop their young, they press against her side,
Their calls of agony not so great a shout
As if she were not there to hear they cried.

I would send her all my love this way,
In a ranting and incompleted poem,
Attempting with industry not as a small child to say,
"Love!" But as a woman not too well or wisely grown.

Somehow in whatever house this gray-eyed one keeps
In haphazard absent-minded disarray,
One ear is tuned to window where the locust Acridiidae
leaps
And to her addresses a private roundelay.

About on tables and sills crowd blooming hypnotized
flowers;
Her left hand tends them, her right holds a political
treatise;
Her notions are Greek-founded, yet laid in present hours,
Concerned and absolute for her country's true increase.

On a dim wall is framed a baby in fine yellowed lace
Upon an ample long-dressed sunlit lap;
A smile of pleasure wreathes the tiny face,
Surfeit of sleep and food and warmth in my crocheted
cap.

When time moved and she came once to visit me,
We had to buy a dozen varied saplings for she said,
"You can't have a yard without a tree!"
From the cellar I got up a pick and a man's stout spade;

The rocks had been created one with the soil
And to make a root-basin properly
Took a half hour's steady toil.
"Here," she said, and grasped the tool, "Let me

Dig that hole. My body's old
And doesn't matter longer. You are young!"
Helpless, half-astonished I stood;
She heaved and chopped, the boulder's flung,

The cave was built forthwith. I would send
Her all my love, knowing she has no patience or place
In her valiant person for tribute. Still I would commend
To her retiring self enormous processionals of praise.

Am I Waiting for a Knock upon the Door?

Am I waiting for a knock upon the door?
Is it death or the next day or a friend or child I'm
        waiting for?
And when I hear it will I rise and lift the latch
And find no one? Will my caller be loneliness come to
        watch
Me stalk about my rooms? I'll draw a chair
And make him welcome saying, Oh where
Have you been? Are you afraid? You must not hide.
And come more often, please. Don't remain outside
Wandering up and down the stair. I hear you sometimes
        in the night
And it disturbs my rest; I've often wanted to invite
You in. Do you ever stand in the shadow at the bookcase?
Am I wrong in mentioning that I've seen your face
Now that we are at last eye to eye? Have you been lost
In my mirror's dark? Now that I've found you, stay,
        dear guest.

The Age of the Flower

Unjealous, you let me touch the flower,
Crouched kissing as if I were its lover,
Which I am, being in the power
Of all small pink roses everywhere living.

This is partly because I know the striving
That took place when all the world was greening,
When forests drowned and reptiles went sleepwalking,
And no bloom was to meet a serpent's eye.

In the room's twilight their mystery
Blazes within their dark corner. The key
Is there. In the fire of the roses does lie
The answer. This is no poem but a prayer.

The Childe to the Tower Came

Men and countries crumble.
All things are lovely in their beginnings.
When he sat across
At that foolish German place
Outside the city (what was its name?)
And ordered small dry
Martinis, one apiece,
(Wanting later to walk in the grass by the river
And then to return to the gallery)
And *preisselbeeren* wrapped in hot thin pancakes.
In the sun-yellow window
The tables were so small one had
To push the dishes together,
And his hand kept touching because of
Being the beginning.
The gaudy-costumed waitress declared that
The president of some dark nation had been shot
And a mob had stoned the ambassador
Who was not yet dead, though near.
Her hand, freckled, trembled pouring the wine,
"Do they want independence in a day!"
The liquid spilled on the fine
White cloth, from her indignation,
In dark ochre drops.
Last week Charlemagne got thrown
Back at the gates of Saragossa (shields and stirrups
    clinked,
The horses' heavy coverings shifted,

And men's brooding faces gazed at the arrow-bristled
walls).
The army was recalled to Saxony due to some revolt.
Now there's news of a disaster in the pass
At the narrow spot on the road from Pamplona
(They say it's but fourteen feet wide)
To St. John Pied de Port
(A thin trumpet wound the last man's falling).
"Damn the Basques, sir," our fierce
Speckle-fingered waitress cried, "when I think
Of all the dukes and Frankish chiefs slain!"
Diffident, he sympathized, "Though it's not
Our crown involved. Or our land. Now is it?
Could you please bring us cigarettes?"
The river grew dark
And the gallery had closed.
Finally because of another engagement of his
We had to leave the inn, and it
Was no longer a beginning.

All Praise to the Virtue Purity

All praise to the virtue Purity!
There is no question of what it is.
It is as exact as the edge of no and yes;
It is the intellectually correct man.
It is or it is not; Purity is sublime.

In Purity is no innocence;
In it is the labor of half-broken-hearted men,
Born to a martyrless time,
Not to be recognized like Savonarola tamed
On the wheel and flung on the cross
And in the Piazza burned;
Or Socrates, impatient: "What's this foolish outcry!"
To those who wept as he was starting to die.

In Purity is no excess, no indulgence, no conceit;
Purity is catholic love;
It is the hind that goes ghostly
Among the dark intertwined boles of dishonesty.

There Is a Beast That Waits Outside the Door

There is a beast that waits outside the door,
Coughs occasionally nothing more,
Makes no bark no threaten no roar,
I fear him so I weep at night.

This menace hidden from all sight,
This mythological parasite,
Has my undoing for his delight;
I stir the fire to make it bound and glow.

I need a blaze to kill all shadow;
Whatever burns on the flames I throw,
And when the fuel is gone into the dark I'll go
To the beast that softly coughs outside the door.

I Am Walking Through Rooms

(To D.R.)

I am walking through rooms calling your name;
The twilight is darkening the corners;
There is nobody here, only your yellow roses;
It is raining and heat hangs like a blanket
Between me and possessions: my bed and my yellow bird
Motionless in his open cage, his shape as vague
As the shapes of your yellow roses looking
Like baby tigers. Where are you now?
I go through rooms naming your name.

Because of the Sisters of Lazarus

The wonder was not that He raised Lazarus.
What was it to Him to be miraculous?
The miracle was that His patience held
And that all the ages dead were not compelled,
Feeling the flame in that so-slowly lifted hand
And that so-tired finger unfolding pained,
That all the moldering dead did not terrified swim
In a tide of monstrous bones and dust toward Him.
"Oh, take ye away," He wept, "the gravestone."
And Mary and Martha and the crowding disbelievers
groaned.
"Come forth now," He sighed. Then around the earth
Where those in stinking graveclothes in their death
Festered, a sudden yearning burned
And nature's laws were almost overturned.
He sensed it and in Him leapt temptation
To end man then and there and to hold Resurrection.
But He so-wearily that patient hand withdrew;
"Loose the bindings," the anger fading, "and let Lazarus
go."

Ask a Silly Question

Ask a silly question get a silly answer;
What is the distance between myself and you?
The length, my love, it takes a full pipe to cinder,
As far as the brilliant eyes of our unborn infants see.
Why do flowers shatter while thorns sting on forever?
Because water is made of ice, my love, and each dove
        from an egg.
Why do men like you live in lovely houses?
Because mahogany is soft, my love, and the late twilight
        green.

When did you find the shoes you were searching after?
Who drowned all those babies when Noah sailed the Ark?
Why is there a sundown? Which woods are yours, my
        darling?
Because all the birds left, my love, and the sky turned
        black.
There's a foolish answer to every foolish question;
If the lipstick on the coffee cup in your house is not mine,
(There's a silly moral to every silly lesson)
Then is our love beginning, my love, or is it at an end?

Get a Silly Answer

Ask a silly question get a silly answer;
How much do I love you? Let me count the ways.
Why do sunsets matter when the colors are conflicting?
Because a cuckoo sings in spring, dear, and gives away its
eggs.
When have you contentment which I cannot seem to
give you?
When it is the time of martyrs, dear, and you are not born
too late.
Where am I to turn to when you say our love is over?
To the forest which is dark, dear, and the gingerbread
house is sweet.
What am I to answer when you say you cannot leave me?
How much do you love me? Can you count the ways?

Prelude

The woman is waiting at her window,
All her attention on the street below
Where in the dusk late shoppers go
To and fro; on the curtain her hand
Barely touches; she will stand
Nearly not breathing, without command
Almost of movement; when the man
Will saunter up the street she will feel
Utterly heavy, a lassitudinous female
Creature; when from the hall her bell
Will peal, she will not move, the wheel
Of her life will halt, the old floor
Under her shoe squeak, and an odor
Come, of a shadowed Greek interior,
Of a Roman hall, of long ages before,
Of the wet brown forest from which man
Walked once; changeless is woman!
She will listen when the ringing is again,
And stir bemused to move and slowly turn
The knob, all surprised, "What? Is it you!"

Out on the Lawn Suddenly

(For D.L.C., deceased 11 Sept. 60)

Out on the lawn in the sun suddenly
I saw it in the newspaper obituary,
And the yellow ball heard me curse
And held still
And rang like a bell,
Ashamed of God.

She'd known some day his heart would quit
And their love be sliced apart
To form her present grief.
In the yellow grass I cursed,
I blasphemed in the worst
Way I knew, so the gray bird that winged
Overhead halted mid-air and began to sing
His horror of God.

Like others I went properly
To say the dead one's goodness and agree
With her on her luck
That she'd had what years she'd had,
But in the door going I said, "Listen,
I cursed when I heard."
Her struck eyes blazed. "I don't believe," she said,
"But if there were a God, I'd damn God."
And the sun was ringing

And the gray bird singing
And behind her I watched God enter the room
And take her in soft enormous arms.

Woman

"Will you never be done?" he said.
The woman was combing her hair.
She nodded, not stirring from where she sat;
The tortoise shell teeth in the burnished strands
Sent music forth plucking the planets like strings,
And making the moon even to sing.
So Chephren walked out on Gizeh's sand
And said he'd have a smallish pyramid built this time.
For good luck he smashed a golden cup
On his way back to her chamber.
"Will you never be done!"
"In a minute." She was in the bath;
She leaned and her knees laved with the cloth,
Then drew it up and her shoulders washed,
While butterflies spun in the sun
And in the shade a jeweled frog sung.
And Miltiades said he'd as well lead the fleet
Of seventy vessels to the Aegean to meet
The Persians and secure the Cyclades.
On his return she was pulling her stockings on,
The seams with care smoothing, one and one,
And bending to fasten the garters.
"I'll be right there,"
Her confidence such that a mountain
Somewhere moved itself somewhere else.
"Won't you ever be done?"
Hadrian made up his mind once and for all
That like Shih Huang Ti he'd build a wall.
He set one across Britain, and next made

Between the Danube and the Rhine a palisade.
And the woman on her couch was sinking,
Her fingers beneath it feeling
For her misplaced sandals.
Painters who peered through her curtains
Worked their colors like slavèd demons.
Poets listening to her sighs
Gave birth to enormous madrigals.
Successful then, toes and heels incasing,
She looped and fastened the slender lacing.
And a Child was born and crucified,
And crusaders marched, and empires died,
And Cromwell dissolved the parliament,
And slaves were freed, an atom rent,
Before she pushed the hangings and left the room,
Going to where he sat alone.
He drew her down upon his knee.
"Are you truly done?" said he.

I'm Trying to Learn How to Die

In shadow stands primeval man,
Brute benighted yet able to die;
In his grave: gods, arrows, meat.
No one has taught me how to die.

It's not coming war that benumbs man;
It's not science but mystery
Within himself that frightens man.
Someone should teach me how to die.

Where in our race of present man
Is someone unterrified to die?
Say you are not? I say you lie.
No use to cry, one has to die.

Tell me, is there Paradise?
Is there Hell? So when I die
There's a place to know that I can go.
I'm trying to learn how to die.

Airmail in Summer

The summer is upon us. Lo.
In the noon streets men scarcely move;
Leaves have curled within themselves,
And the insects are holding their breath.
My hand on the limp white curtain is dewed;
I don't know what book of poems I hold,
Am undesirous of sleep or love or food.
Summer is on us again. Lo.

Are you already in Italy?
I recall how the Milanese close their doors
And go to lie on beds of stone,
To listen as water falls from mossy cherubs' mouths.
Above their piazzas the sun is a cauldron
Tipping slowly, as it is now doing
Here in Washington. Are you yet in Florence?

Outside Arezzo, in the Etruscan country,
Past the blackbird leaning on Dante's cheek
And pigeons bathing in madonnas' veils,
The wheat fields are littered with poppies!
White oxen with wilted flowers braided about their brows
Stand before the shrouded women who turn the straw
With slow forks of wood. Lo, the summer.

The hot pot of the sun boils over once again;
The heat falls thickly onto everyone.

I can nearly not move my hand through it
To my hair to push it moist from my face.
Are you planning to return by ship or air?
I read old dead poets, Vergil and Ovid
And Catullus: *What a woman says*
To an eager lover, write it on running water, on air.
Do go to see the white beasts in the evenings!
In a way I wish I were there,
For lo, here is nothing but summer.

The Importance of Mirrors

The woman in her room is standing at the mirror.
What is she seeing? The way the wind tears her hair
As it blows through the window? No. Does she hear
Something? The cry of the old hen in the yard

Like all of them out there, from wedding card
To chopping-block, dust on their wings endured
From the leaping roosters? No. She has not heard.
Well, do her white nostrils then catch the scent

From the bedpost behind her exuding faint,
(It's a virgin's cot, originally meant
For a maidenhead's taking, its boards felled luxuriant
With flowers and bees)? Does she smell it? No, nor taste

Nor feel what's physically about. She has no age, is lost
In the glass, where all her years has querying gazed
At child or wife or hag. She is the host,
Herself her guest. The mirror is her open door.

Sometimes I Feel the Envious Dead Crowd Near

(For W.M.)

Sometimes I feel the envious dead crowd near
When the living become too much for them to endure
Longer; I sense the movement as they stir,
Uneased by so much vitality, a little pained,
In their peace disturbed, down in the counterpart land
Where they are, slow and dark, where boulders stand
For clouds, and roots repeat the patterns of our trees'
Branches, waving weighted in the netherworld's breeze,
Where under our colored flowers grow theirs like black
lace.

Today a friend said, "May I come to sit in your room
And speak out—you can play your guitar—some problem
Bothering me? It's not necessary that you listen."
I felt the dead rustle then! I used once to believe
When I sensed their presences against my sleeve,
That their need for my help made them misbehave.
"What is it?" I would whisper, "is there an action undone
That I can do for you to give you rest? Have you forgotten
To take something you need?" They'd be silent again.
I have argued with them up and down for years that way,
Trying to lay them again in their own country,
Until I grew to associate them with love and joy:
Those brought them up! Like the time the shouting
children

Went in spinning cartwheels and handsprings through
the rooms!
"Ohhh," sighed the shades in protesting unison.

I think the most troublesome are the too recent dead,
Not yet used to the newness of eternity, somewhat afraid
Of the different landscape that is theirs now, carpeted
With slow swaying tendril roots of grass,
Balancing pebbles for bees; there are rivers that pass
Silvery in unfamiliar patterns. I want to ease
These dead, as you reason with a child
Who has lost a loved toy, "Don't look at us; in a while
You will have forgotten." They never hear my call at all.

Nonage

When I was born my father tied it by the door,
Giving it a pat and saying, "There,"
The creature with a golden mane and dreadful smile,
Caparisoned; its jeweled hoofs struck fire.
I have had to feed it through the years
And clean up its dung and brush its silk hair down
And wash by hand its rich trappings.
And all the while I've feared to look
Upon its open beautiful brow
And into its eyes that glittered like
The wandering planets of the Zodiac.
Oh, but its voice mocked me; it was terrible!
I grew to hate the sound as I came bashful,
Unwilling before it. Within the house
My father was telling my mother, "When
She is ready she will ride it.
You will see." It was my eighteenth birthday.
I leapt among the velvet and the bells and rode away.

Visit

(For N.F.)

In the park men doff iron broad-brimmed hats and green
Horses rear under them. Hot stone eagles scream
While overhead in a yellow despairing pool
The sun is melting. Why is it never cool
In your city! I had thought to find you alone
When I rang your bell. But that placid dark woman
Was there and would not go, spoiling it. Now I cannot
        return
For nearly a year. At the station I learn
That the trains are running late. In me sorrow's bud
Explodes in a slow bitter flower of finitude.

At Twenty

(To John Carl Steichen)

The foreign soil is dusted on your shoes,
You, these many months gone, returned.
The arrogance of conquest is in your stance
As you hurl the door to and enter my domain.
Your fierce voice startles, used to a small son
Soberly erecting erector sets, not even swearing,
Conscientious, religious, within my hearing,
A gentle child! And I employing strong words at times
In a temper, being amazed and thinking you tender
And alien. You were a still boy, who now come
To my room with a loud sound like laughter. Why, I
wonder,
Can I scarcely touch your fresh hard face? Stranger!

This evening I glance across to where in a chair
Your cradled guitar makes odd tunes from some land
Where women shield their faces and men go hand in
hand,
And you tear open black figs large as oranges,
The pink flesh hot and sweet and sensuous.
You have lifted veils; you have with those men
Taken wine resinous, half-warm. There is brine
In your new beard, sinewy your different hand.
In the shadow your mouth glints telling of a dragon
And mermaids, of swine to men and men to swine.

Rocked on my knees in fever were you once mine?
With mouth then like a flower from which now I turn?

You do not know nor ever shall, tall one,
How frequently to my angel I mention
Your name in a bargaining fashion. Let, I pray, this rebel son
Outlive me! no longer any visible part to him.

In My Room Your Red Roses Are Unbeautifully Dying

In my room your red roses are unbeautifully dying!
I have been one on whom lovers at times
Have shredded red and white and rose roses in full blow;
I have been one who stood aside to watch
An uncle, wounded-eyed, tearing apart roses
And hurling them in fistfuls at his father's lowering bier.

Your red roses in the jar are too old;
When they came to my room a week ago, blushing
cherubs,
I thought little of them. Now they are terrible
Reproachful angels, who stand gathered tightly
To themselves. I touch one and it trembles within
In a soft frightful way, its petals unfalling.

Your red roses in my room age before my eyes,
Mournful, black-rimmed, wrinkled as Villon's whores.
I want to throw them in the trash bin with death
And sorrow and all dark mythological emotion. Instead
I stand helpless before them, shifting my feet
Enduring the unbeautiful dying of your red roses!

Across the Street Outside the Window

Across the street outside the window,
Exploding in a rose-mauve glow,
The letters of a neon theatre sign
Match the aging colors of the sky.
The sleepy drivers flick on their lights;
The traffic in slowed rows moves;
The city readies itself for night.

Long since were a father and a mother,
To them all duty tuned, all need, all prayer;
And a dog, a shepherd mongrel,
With whom, curled on the floor in the cold upper hall,
Hearing the parents talking over dishes in some distant
room,
After a purple-tinted play-drugged even,
One fell asleep, him gripped in love-swooned arms.

About the buildings draws a rough black curtain,
As God departs somewhere, his rosy robe taken.
A distant siren screams alarum bit by bit;
Children on the walk below argue for the sake of it;
A pair of drunken dangering men
Reel, crying gibberish past the burning neon,
Wearing their violence like rusted swords.

Must one turn old, love itself distort?
Must good be evil? Must time, like the ravening night-
bird,
Come us to wound, his prey,
Tearing flesh from bones, eyes from the light of day?
One ploughs about the mind for reasons,
Harking back and back and back to other seasons
Until one comes on hungered-for childhood rose-glowed
skies.

I Have Two Mirrors

I have two mirrors; one in the hand,
The other one behind me stands.
In this the pale features behold,
In that the dark hair is told.
The diminishing images disappear,
Childhood and age juxtaposed unclear.

Faces and hair, hair and faces,
Cases with lids, and lids on the cases,
Neatly fitted, bodies and souls,
The babies roar when the thunder rolls,
The graves gape open and you fall in fast.
The past is future and the future just passed!

Swan Song

The high flying bird that caused the crash of a United Air Lines Viscount Friday was identified as a swan. The plane plummeted into a woods, killing all 17 persons aboard. —*News item*

When the time is come for me to die,
I wish that those who think of me might mourn,
The cause of her death was a swan flying high!

Out of the sky seventeen were torn,
Wingless unwitting Icaruses,
Stripped and astonished and earthward borne

Down into autumn woods and death,
The cause of this incident a holy bird,
Sailing on a mute and gentle journey south

And stopped by The Ancient of Days. Below a world
Observed the flames and wondered at a clear cry
Through the bellowing of the wreckage overheard.

Someone Should Say It to You, Daughter

(To Karlen Paula Steichen)

Someone should say it to you, daughter: love.
Daughter, I loved you when you were three,
The way I loved the golden spaniel pup,
Who scampered sunny-tempered on the porch.
You never cried, you laughed;
You never walked, you ran;
You never liked, you loved;
You never spoke, you sang.

Someone should say it to you, daughter: love.
Daughter, I love you best now at nineteen,
The lines of worry there where you have frowned,
Your quiet way of going from a room.
You cry too much, you laugh too much,
You walk too much, and run;
You like too much, you love too much,
You speak too much, and sing.

Yesterday I saw in you no part of me,
Although I knew that you were of my blood
And had my smile and had my mother's eyes.
Sister, today you stood before the glass
And took the comb and ran it through your hair

And looked into your eyes and there saw me
And my mother and her mother and hers.
Let someone say it, daughter, sister: love.

Bravery

The deep sound of your laugh has shaken me;
It broke across the evening-darkened porch,
Where sun and shade today have made their way
Through blinds and over boards; the sound came coarse
As from some old-time man, who in the noon
Walked the town streets when the Black Plague
Had frightened to death all small souls.

My conversation halted at the rough sound;
What was I saying? lost in a sudden dream of another
man,
Who threw on armor to wear about his nude breast,
And mounting a charger, rode to a hot brown field,
Where by the time the sun had fallen in a red pool
At the end of day, he died or survived; in either case
That sound through the land broke upon the twilight.

Sonnet

(To W.P.)

Why always do I remember what I need not
Remember, forgetting the rest? In twilight I found
Myself awake on my couch, half-drowned
In some old dream. Aloud I tried but had forgot
Your name. Looking for it, I came on a great white
Cat which wandered from under a table without sound
In wherever your house is, somewhere in this town.
Why should I easily remember your cat?

Are your eyes blue or brown? Your hair
Light or dark? Do you carry a walking cane?
Do you come riding a horse or driving a car?
Have we met in a dark wood? Was there rain?
I recall the weave of the cloth of your collar
And the set of your bones when you move. And that
feline.

Maybe 15 mph for the Candlestickmaker

(To Jean Pierre Steichen,
deceased 9 Dec. 44)

And the oily greedy unpleasantly nonsmelly
Handlers of dead bodies,
The undertakers,
Took my good grandfather
After his quiet death
Upon which he had placed his blessing;

They bore him,
Whose sly driving-horse was an ex-race horse,
Who always commanded me to overtake every car ahead,
Who delighted in the smooth speed of the ambulance
That rushed him to his last bed;

These stupids interminably bore his empty shell
At fifteen miles per hour
To his grave.

Sonnet

I think perhaps you will knock sometime in a dream
And I will find a heap of trembling flowers
Piled at my doorside; they will all velvet seem
And made of paycocks' wings, of darkled colors,
Rubied. Oh, I will spend the hours
Gathering them in. (Wasted, I'll tell myself, these
blooms
On me!) And beneath their opiate stores
Like a moth will flutter a letter which comes
From you who thought, wooing, of me in your rooms,
As some busy Pericles who took pause
To think of milky thighs, of lips and perfumes,
Before again remaking Athens' cause.

Let you sometime in a dream bring me a few
Flowers; and perhaps instead of the message, you?

It Is Nearly May

In haste I ran out the door
Tonight, having glimpsed the moon over
The hill through the window glass,
Slipping fast like a grape from a skin.
She glows as if within
Herself a bulb were screwed for Halloween,
The plug pushed in a socket someone found
Among the trees in the ground
Of the hill over there.

I can hear the dropping of the tulip skins
From the wounded stiffened stems
In the dark. It comes
Over the noise of cars which run
On the wet cement one by one a quarter mile from
My yard, swishing. The petals turned brown
The other night when a frost came down
And put the finger of death
To them, sprung out of untended earth.
The old bulbs had been planted in a mad
Frenzy seven years ago. They were
His most expensive stock, the best,
Our hardware man said, the finest.
Then no less would do for my garden! Now
They shiver imprisoned in a row
Letting their hurt petals go.

And meanwhile lightless on the hill
The elliptical tangerine still
Stares at me as if aware of my being here
With the tulips. Tonight I plunged
Fast from the house when
I saw her. I had been
Reading a book and had seen
The face in the square of window loom
Like a long lost loved uncle whom
One had forgot, and then unpredicted, came home again.

Lover, I Feel a Pain in the Land of the Heart

Lover, I feel a pain in the land of the heart
When you turn delighted and speak the ways
Of me and that you are pleased, when you praise
White armpits and one's drowned eyes.

Lover, why does something within begin to tally days,
Like old wives who gather apples in a red sun
And list jealous harvests? Some day will come
From you a sharp word; one dies from

Knowing of it, from that expectation!
The fear pierces like that of heights, or a chart
Of unknown seas before, a profound hurt.
Lover, bravely celebrate me before we ever part.

The Chief and Well-Learned Lesson

I thought when I was in my burning youth
That with the aging of my heart I would grow calm,
A gentle person, wise, serene. The truth
Is: life's but an education in the ways of pain.

There was that old woman, my mother, out
In the barn checking the cows to ascertain
Who the baby bull had settled this fall, who not,
And fell trampled in the straw, subsequently
Denying the blood and bruise, "This year
Every one, even the heifer, got caught!"

There was that older man, my grandfather,
Who slapped my helping hand in wrath
From him, tumbling, spilling the milk
Over the tray, "Christ, I'll do it myself!"
And I was observant while the heart broke
Dutiful, curious, attentive of life.

But one thing spoken made me think
I'd never be the same again but spend
Much time in heart-contracted sulking.
You said, "If I had but met you when
I was young and in my first wild prime!"
Burning once, I might have shut my ears.
Now, adjusted to hurt, I take my time,
The chief and well-learned lesson of my years.

It Is April!

April: it is the season of galloping cows;
Heavy-thighed farm women are kneeling in wet fields
Tending something green and small that hides
In the brown untidy furrows. It is April!
The crooked pear tree drops white blooms.
The bull sniffs and lowers a curly-thatched head;
He digs a forehoof in the sod and roars with passion
Which arrived before he was aware, and startled him
From where he cudded, lost in winter drowsing.

And the boy born in a ditch, Vergil, listens
To the white Mantuan bull, and in the distance
To springtime screaming of the Gonzaga dukes' stallions;
He leans against the budded olive tree which is a serpent,
Carvèd and still; he sighs when the air stirs;
He senses the bestiality of nearby snoring haymakers,
The suffering underlying a sun-drenched farm cottage.

And the Galilean woman in long blue robes in the crowd
Is not hearing *all* of the words of the man on the slope,
Who talks continually into a whirling perfumed wind;
She understands that he sways the people from stoning
him;
She feels his limp stainèd form already in her arms,
Unfastened from the tree against the storm-rolling April
sky.

The horses of the soldiers nicker in the city below,
The farmers are stripping spring-full udders of cows.

A cherry-flower touched wind sweeps down upon
Virginia farmers' fields; there the women as if in prayer
Have fallen slowly before the sprouted seeds
In the pattern of the ages, as they always will! April.

The Unclasping

(To W.S.)

Did you write to me and mention love?
Love is summer. Here the foghorns roar;
Here the winter drags upon the year,
A stubborn old beast that's fastened to the throat
Of spring, and will not let her go,
Will not let softness spread and change the look
Of tenseness everyone wears, mirroring desire.
Spring? It will never come. Nor love again.
The cold old lake remains a meadow of ice;
I heard in the streets that for the first time
In old men's memory the ice froze clear across.

How the winter growls and holds its grip,
While I try recalling summer and cannot!
Couples walk apart, their breath a-steam.
Was it ever summer? No. Did that pale disc
Ever boil over, pouring heat in heavy swirls
Upon the pavements of this now ice-bound town?
No. And I cannot name the name of love.
Was there ever love? No. Love is summer,
And the entire city is holding its breath,
Waiting on the unclasping of the fangs
Of winter, on the turning loose of spring.
Will you write to me again and mention love?

On War

The rain has halted which beat with wet strong wings,
And we walk in the cold sweet air by our Potomac's water;
Nature's storm is over and tongue-tied with languor
I cannot say what I most wish to know:
Lover, what is the color of your eyes?

Darius, bloodied, died in his chariot,
Spear-riddled on that noisy plain,
In the palm of a hundred and twenty thousand Persians
slain;
I hear that stinking Alexander chokes now in a drunk
fever
In his fair palace; I trust he's done for;
I pray this be once and for all an ending of war!

Babylon's river flings itself in trembling gray-green tides;
The city's battlements behind us shine in dark glazed
shrouds
That mirror the falling of all the empires
To the damned Macedonian commanders.
All day I can wonder only on your eyes' color.
(Women are this way; we blindly make our different pain
Which seems small, insisting upon it with minds beyond
man's
Comprehending.) The churning fumbling post-rain
Clouds above resemble battle, and in the west there

Where yellow flare of sunset blazes, one would think
That whelp Ptolemy already had burned his path into
Egypt,
Or Uncle Billy Sherman's bastards swung
Their lighted pitch clubs into farmers' barns, or some
Pilot struck his match to Hiroshima.

Lover, let us go home. *Your eyes at last*
Look suddenly on me! They are honeyed as the color of
bees;
Green and black and amber-flecked
And hot and wild and brown,
They are not yet turned away from me to the coming
storm.

Written on the Death of a Poet

Let all Christian men fall to their knees
And sun-idolaters and heretics,
Believers, nonbelievers. Let all these
Raise their voices in pagan keen.
Robert Frost goes once again to earth!

See the branches of all the trees
Whip themselves in the wind that cries;
See the soil opened in a fresh-digged pile
Writhe and refuse to lie still.
Robert Frost goes once again to earth!

Near nine decades he walked upon her fields
And said his say in a steady argument
To celebrate his marriage to her,
Who now takes him upon her grievèd heart.
Robert Frost goes once again to earth!

See the sun withdraw within the whirled clouds
And all the disturbed elements misbehave.
Let living men mark a cross on their calendars
That on this day a certain event occurred.
Robert Frost goes once again to earth!

I Am Listening for a Step upon the Stair

I am listening for a step upon the stair;
The sun through the window blazons on the wood;
The dishes are half-done, soap bubbles glint;
The creaking hands of time have slowed and stopped.

When I am grown and wise all this will change,
And the clickety-clack of eternity never halt;
But today I am twenty and the bird sings in the tree,
And the child within me sighs and rolls and sleeps.

Outside his step has come upon the stair,
And bird and sun and child and time unite;
I dry my hands on the towel and go to the door,
And the wheels of reality again begin to turn.

The Pretext

Now while nobody's looking tell me quick,
Why must flowers always have to praise?
Why must the sea by a ship appear so black?
Why must guitar strings make their particular noise,

Shaking me, kissing the stem? Why must the clock move?
Why must babies cry when they come from sleep?
Why must birds sound ever as if they grieve?
While nobody notices, dear, say the answer quick,

Hurting me. What makes the cat lie still
In the evening sun? What makes the gold light come
Upon your face which seems allegorical,
Non-god, non-beast, non-fable, non-human?

Your pretext for answering is me, so speak
Now while nobody's looking and tell me quick.

The Teen-agers

I saw three virgins by the road
Who had been walking in the wood.

They were sitting on a culvert edge
Underneath a privet hedge.
Their jeans and socks were ripped by a briar;
The wind had mussed their hair;
Their lipstick was all licked away.
None of them was a day
Past fifteen.
Their eyes daydreamed,
Tear-swimming. They had
No notion why they were sad
Or why on this fine sunny day
There was nothing more to each other to say.

They looked like three nuns in a row,
Going where they had been told to go.

The Calf of the Black Cow

The calf the black cow had inside of her
Refused to be ordinarily birthed.
He had grown grotesque within her natural womb,
Like some noble bewitched thing foredoomed.
The black cow fell upon her knees in wonder
Near midnight; the twisted rope hung from her,
Which told the farmer the channel for her young
Had opened; but the child would not come;
Heavy-skulled, furry, to the womb's walls he clung,
Though his mother bawled and in the barnyard flung.

At dawn the veterinary leaned against a tree
And aimed and spit tobacco and drowned a fly
And rolled his sleeves and his fingers greased
And the knife bent double within his fist.
Up to his bloodied shoulder in the cow
He did to death the thing which wrongly grew;
And when he went to the trough to wash his arm,
The bull calf lay dismembered on the lawn;
And from the severed monstrous curly-locked head,
Huge eyes gazed liquid, gentle, enchanted.

The black cow sighed and came to lick the face of her
son,
Who had made his stand and fought his war and won.

I Choose Now Lonely to Ring the Bell

I choose now lonely to ring the bell
Of mourning for the homes to me lost
And my abandoned children. I toll for Baby Nell,
For Betsey in round blue cap, for Mary Jane; sawdust
And plaster to others, but to me the child,
Receptacles for love that would have rent
Me were they not there to shelter it. When told
To place each doll upon a shelf, without dissent
I obeyed; comprehending Corinthians, I
Knew the obligation to put away such things.

My houses too were forsook; one a tree
Platform amid green grandeur with rope strings
Of ladder leading up. How can I speak
Enough of it, it was so elegant? As was
One carved in rooms of sand, and one a stick-
And-straw hut, thatched with colored fall leaves.
Oh, I seem to have spent my young years
In household fantasies! Until it appears the sky'd
Plummeted finally around my ears, the sensible fears
Of my primer mate, Chicken Little, justified.

Missionary

It was early in my city, in the doubting time
Between midnight and morning before light had come,
When suddenly awakening a memory pressed
Of a quick dream and yet not one, overtaking,
Of a long faint call the dark shaking,
Which I knew to be personal, to myself addressed;
Over the walls and half-hid roofs, it reached distinct.

All windows remained dark save one
Across the paved court where some unknown
Old woman white-begowned and capped,
Her cup at her dowdy table supped;
Familiar to me as the stunted tree
Along the street which was not intimate,
A courteous salute on greeting that was all. Straining,
I leaned my eyes into the coming dawn for more.

There was only the morning wounding the night
And it ruined, dying, the question remaining,
Was I needed somewhere? Had someone called?
Was there nowhere, ready, in this day for me to go!

Dust

I slept in a tomb round and red,
In the land of my mother I made my bed,
Until one day she set me free
And I became a devotee
Of rain and tree and earth and sky;
I ran and leapt and bragged that I
Would never die but now I'm back
Within a country long and black,
Awaiting another natal day
When I can again go out to play.

Let Us Suffer Alone, Lover

Across the room we face each other;
You are past the tiny Czechoslovak cups of strong coffee
And the used crystal, the burned pale candles which
crowd
Upon the small table draped with yellowed linen.
I am trying to tell you that I cannot be owned
Any more than you can own the tree that is in your yard
Or the dog that is in your house
Or the wife that may some day inhabit your bed.
All have their wish to be recognized by your praise,
Your command, or your hand upon her breast.
But that is enough.

We must not imprison each other.
Cut off my arms and I will run from you;
Take my legs and I will still be free;
Pluck out my eyes and close my mouth,
With your dagger spear from me my heart,
Upon my blood I shall carry my liberty,
And when you have drained that you will still see
The uncrumbled wraith of me denying you.
We must release each other;
Let me go; I will return. Let us suffer alone, lover,
In the primeval unselfish way.

The Visitor

Returned this year to the old tall house
Where my childhood was,
Where ever since I've lived my dreams;
Where I've swayed afraid
In a nightmare conceived
Of a long reaching staircase
And wide huge angry rooms of space;
Where a sled drives through snow
Repetitively in a place I know;
Where a peaceful fence slopes
And running round a corner my dog speaks.

Wonder if I've laid my dreams
At last, for the old house is
Of its old nobility stripped.
Silent, bare, like a rotted grave-post
It stands. The worst
Is that it's shrunk.
In my mind of childhood I'd made it grow
Larger each year
Like my grandfather's peaches
And cherries, remembered from Luxembourg.
My aunts took him back once
Partly to stop his stories of the immense
Size of the fruit, to make him see them as they were,
Knotted and tiny and imperfect.

Wonder if it were wise to go,
And enter square boxed toy rooms
And pass white small unfamiliar doors
Laid out in the same proper pattern. But so
Diminished! Up the short staircase whose walls
Grew in while I was not
There to watch. The falling dust
Smothers old loved cats and dogs
And pet crows that raced
And flew in the sun and gloom
Of my life a short while ago.

The Drunk Stepped on the Streetcar

The drunk stepped on the streetcar
Straight from the mouth of hell;
His head swung like the sanctus bell,
The holy holy holy tool;
Passengers faces had frozen aware,
Eyes masked themselves from his despair;
He hurled a fist groaning, "Curse you all";
His dark eyes hunted demoniacal.
He would whisper his secret truth for sure,
And it composed the general fear,
The pervading thrill a-thirst to hear,
As children who gather at top of stair
To net and savor each word of the quarrel.
But all he whispered from his personal horror
Was, "I am a man," the rage being there,
As if he'd warred with ridicule;
"I am a man." He slapped down his dare
And I for one saw the rare jewel.

The Ballad of Woman

He took a spear and drove it in her breast;
Under her broken ribs it came to rest
Within her red and bravely beating heart;
Shaft broken, the heavy iron grew one and part
To her tamed flesh; she wore its weight so
All her victory became that none should know.

Upon a stirrup his gay boot he pressed,
And bridle of his great white beast carest;
Not seeing his lady standing all in red,
He rode her down in dust of the road's bed;
When he'd gone his way she rose and washed,
And returned to castle where she lightly laughed.

In her room she knelt at her prie-dieu,
And all marveled at this lady's piety.

Lazarus

The blind man on the corner of F and 7th sings,
Around his neck a guitar from an ancient string,
And by the iron fence his cup is kept where rings
A dropping coin occasionally;
His voice is not too like an angel's yet
Thinking of darkness, it is enough.
Who posts the city's cripples or
Do they post themselves?
Outside the five-and-dime the legless man
With elephantine smile collects his silver.
Beside the music shop is one
So twisted you would not believe it, for
His head is nearly wrung to the pavement floor
Where it stays; he is smileless, though it may
Be simply due to his deformity.
These people are like cautions set about
By some sermonizing deity, wanting men to say,
There but for God's grace, begs me.

Destiny

That fatted calf, it knew. It
Heard the father's shout
And its pure knowing heart
Shrank. The running feet
The old man's pant
Down the path unable longer to wait
For his approaching child, the downcast
Prodigal long considered lost.
The little calf against the post
Of the stall quivered, felt
The knife long before it smote
And life throbbed quietly from its snowy throat.

Christmas Carol

There are four apples on my window sill;
In fancy: three holy, one apocryphal.
I call them: *Son, Father, Dove.* Stumped,
I cannot name the last, unesthetically humped
Red-black below the chilly pane. My triad unison
I tell again: *Dove, Father, Son.*

They lean against each other, comfortable, merry;
And now I recognize the fourth: *Old Harry,*
Who's come to say a plague on my Christmas season,
To assault my Trinity with ambiguous reason
And demonstrate that Three have need of four,
As Heaven will link to Hell forevermore.

The Giraffe

Smith said, "I cannot bear to look
On that tall beast with the snakish neck
And bespeckled body. I'm feeling sick;
My eardrums throb. It's true!"

Smith did his best his courage to screw,
For he liked very much to visit the zoo;
With aplomb a fierce yellow cat he would view
And okapis bravely stare down.

But that twinkling feeble eye of brown
Was what made Smith say he'd never come
To the park again. He went straight home
And lay down, afraid. Who knows why?

Doctor, doctor, will Smith die?
It would be a catastrophe!

See-saw Marjorie Daw

It braced its feet and pecked and then its wings spread
slow,
There in the sun in front of the Sunday-moving car,
An idle scavenging blue-black silly crow
On the highway feeding at some rabbit's guts and fur.

But the tiny glinting eyes strayed quick on me and mine,
And the day was the sun was the hot light was the crow
was doom!

On the Sixth Day of April This Year

On the sixth day of April this year
I picked a blade of grass
From a yard in Denver,
Colorado. It was
A dull and dusted spear,
Sprouted in soot, fed by fear
Of trampling feet,
Not knowing sun at all or a clear
Swept look that sky can have.
And back behind the cave
The city made, I could hear
Mountains bellowing.
I heard them I swear
Under a sun yellowing.

I picked a twig of sage two days before
On a mountainside on April four,
Near Fort Collins, Colorado, this same year.
I'd been driven there
In an ancient car
By a young college pair.
He lean in tight jeans; she pregnant, fair,
White teeth, red lips, gold hair.
The trees whistled and whispered and

I crushed the brittle gray-green sage.
The wind was using the pines for a tongue.
I smelled the sage on my hands;
Then saw the small-balled dung
Of mule deer. "Look here!"
And before a crow could call
Or a magpie fall
Into a fir or a ponderosa pine,
The trio of deer walked into the clear
Before the trees on the mothering mountain.
One a young buck with antlers shy,
Two does with great dark eyes.
With watchful step they passed by.
Already the tall young mountain man
Had shot all three
With his camera slung
On his arm. And was stalking like a fourth,
Slowly after them down the north
Slope, as if compelled. The sky yelled
And raced around the snow-stained peaks
And dashed its light in stripèd streaks
On everything. On the boy who was moving
Like a muscled wild thing, shoving
The deer before him. You understood
He could stroke their long ears if he would;
They would stand and never move.
I heard the mountains.
I heard the mountains bellow
Under the sky of yellow.

I folded my piece of sage
In a handkerchief and climbed in a cage

On a later date,
On April eight
This year,
On a railway train that rattled and battled
And shuttled and bumped
And swayed across a continent;
Eastward, downward, to Washington.
In a box of bricks
Under a tree of sticks
Where a lonely starling shrieks,
I opened the cloth.
From the green-gray stuff the scent came up.
Three deer, the buck and both
Dark-eyed does walked through the walls.
I crumpled the sage leaves in the cup
Of my palms and laid them to my face.
The deer stood
Watchful in a green-glowing aspen wood
In my house in Washington.
Mountains muttered.
Mountains roared.
They bellowed.
I heard them, I swear.
I heard the mountains bellow
Under my walls of yellow.

Plaisir d'Amour

We quarreled and the pale sun gleamed paler;
We quarreled and the autumn leaf that balanced
On its branch ready to fall
Could not fall but waited for a reason.
The causes of our quarrel were changeless
As we are; your jealousy across the town chimneys
Assaults me; my weeping is thick and strong;
The leaves being balanced everywhere unfalling.

The taxi driver waits, hearing an ambulance shriek
Louder than a shriek should be; around the corner
The red beast brakes beside a mess
Of disassembled crumpled halted cars,
And a prone figure over which the crowd bends
Gasping, the prone one stiller than still.
And the leaves started to fall all the way home
And the sun burned and I remembered we quarreled.

Restoration

Rilke, you gave my angel back to me.
Angel, you come again behind my shoulder;
I had forgot. You stand in the old proximity;
I hear you breathe, you are bolder
Than once, when you made no sound;
But then you were my doll, my plaything,
And I never felt the darkness, the wound.
How you need me! with beating wing
Rushing to see if I have called,
If I have startled from my chair,
Crying, "My jewel, my emerald,
My dear! Are you still here?"

And if you are not because you are busy elsewhere,
I make no complaint, knowing the fault of women
Is to smother love with their attentions. I require
Of you nothing, I hold my white arms down
And cross them on my breast so when you arrive
My tranquility and ease reassures
You that you can rest your tired head upon my love
Forever, angel, needing my pity more than I need yours.

The Tree

In spring a dogwood can be
A most extraordinary tree,
Its white blossoms free
Of all support, balanced there
In the heated twilight air
Outside the kitchen window screen,
Held in the hurtful green of spring.
The back yard lawn has been shorn between
Untidy clover clumps
And matted tortuous molepath bumps.

Here is the hiss of broiling meat,
The scent, the felt wintry creak
Of the old house's bones.
Here the cat yawns,
Turns itself, and sleeps.
The coffee urn steams;
The brown odor seeps to the window,
Out into the dusk that gleams
Purple, denoting coming showers.

The black branches seem now
Dissolved; the floating
White flowers anchored by unseen
Strings against the young painful green.

On Waking to a Lion's Roar

O Splendid One, your golden mythological voice
Rolls over the centuries and the spring-green tree tops
Into my room. I feel your crouching stance,
Mane lowered and eyes in embers, coughing, gasping
Your statements into the primordial light of dawn.

Your forest paws pace out into the cold floored yard
Which is your barren jungle and your realm;
Disdainful is your gesture, padding to the tree,
Your tail like a muscled ball bat, straight and up,
The urine flung in a stream of male hauteur.

Your throated fury comes again, compounded of Rome
And Rousseau's Dream and Egyptian plaques. With no
knowledge
Of your transplantation, O Beautiful King,
You stand with fiery mystic eyes and understand no bars,
And announce your being, Proud One, Primitive Deity!

The Accident

Forced by broken ribs to contemplation,
I thought of how it would be to be dead,
Not lying here folded in a great white bed,
But cased in a box and under a stone instead.

I thought of all my lively filaments
That now are stretched and smashed to cause me pain,
Dissolving quietly in autumn rain,
Falling apart to dust and air again.

I thought of my bones' responsiveness,
How easily they manage in my skin,
Linked by harmonious cartilage within
The fabulous frame of my skeleton.

I thought of my blood's warm tranquility,
If caught by the blow that surprised my ribs in two,
Cooling gradually to a temperature all new,
Thickening, disintegrating, until ashes too.

I thought with pride of my brain's perfection,
How it lies delicate within my head,
Convoluted, beautiful, veined red,
Wondering on how it would be to be dead.

I thought of that most innate part of me,
That unperceivable essence I admire,
And how tangibly it would not expire,
But redistribute its fine ineffable fire.

Great Lake of My Childhood

Great Lake of my childhood, dangerous and beautiful,
Will you never let me go?
Tonight again you come into my dream,
Churning and foaming, and almost drowning me,
And hurling me upon the shore.

Fabulous, treacherous, mystical, half-tamed beast,
Stay out of my spellbound dreams!
Let me live in peace away from you.
I thought the ache of childhood love
Must diminish when I long since went away.

Dear Great Lake, let me go!
In dreams I walk in sandied bathing suit
Along your sunsetting shore,
The pool of the dying orb spreading to make
A path that follows my progress like a scarlet finger.
All this in broken-hearted dreams.
Dear lovely memory, let me go!

Dear Love I Said to You

(For B.C.)

Dear love, I said to you from in the dream,
Say what makes the willow tree so green,
Say what makes the light on pale skin gleam,
Say while we lie together in the dream.

Your mouth on mine I heard your heart repeat,
The willow's roots are long and dark and sweet,
The pale light is the space where voices meet.
Then where is love? I heard my quick heart beat.

Love, you said, is of its own self wove,
It is not us; there is no act to prove.
In its green time this thing will choose to move,
And then into the dream stood love.

Index

About the Author

Helga Sandburg is the author of three novels, *The Wheel of Earth, Measure My Love* and *The Owl's Roost.* Her most recent work was *Sweet Music,* a book of family reminiscence and song. Miss Sandburg is also the author of four books for children, *Blueberry, Joel and the Wild Goose, Gingerbread* and *Bo and the Old Donkey,* published by The Dial Press.